Flowers

by Gail Saunders-Smith

Photo: Bleeding-Heart

Content Consultant:
Deborah Brown, Horticulturist
University of Minnesota Extension Service

SUPPORT
FOR SCHOOLS

Pebble Books are published by Capstone Press
151 Good Counsel Drive, P.O. Box 669, Mankato, Minnesota 56002
http://www.capstone-press.com

Copyright © 1998 Capstone Press. All rights reserved.
No part of this publication may be reproduced in whole or in part, or stored in a retrieval system, or transmitted in any form or by any means, electronic, mechanical, photocopying, recording, or otherwise, without written permission of the publisher.
For information regarding permission, write to Capstone Press,
151 Good Counsel Drive, P.O. Box 669, Dept. R, Mankato, Minnesota 56002.
Printed in the United States of America.

2 3 4 5 6 07 06 05 04 03 02

Library of Congress Cataloging-in-Publication Data
Saunders-Smith, Gail.
Flowers/Gail Saunders-Smith.
p. cm.
Includes bibliographical references (p. 23) and index.
Summary: Simple text and photographs depict the parts of flowers and their pollination.
ISBN 1-56065-769-3
1. Flowers—Juvenile literature. 2. Flowers—Fertilizers—Juvenile literature. [1. Flowers.] I. Title
QK653.S28 1998
575.6—dc21 98-5049
CIP
AC

Note to Parents and Teachers

This book describes and illustrates the parts of flowers and how flowers grow. The close picture-text matches support early readers in understanding the text. The text offers subtle challenges with compound and complex sentence structures. This book also introduces early readers to expository and content-specific vocabulary. The expository vocabulary is defined in the Words to Know section. Early readers may need assistance in reading some of these words. Readers also may need assistance in using the Table of Contents, Words to Know, Read More, Internet Sites and Index/Word List sections of the book.

Table of Contents

Pistil
Stamens
Petals
Sepals

The flower is the part of the plant that makes seeds. A flower has four parts. They are the sepals, petals, stamens, and pistil.

Photo: Wood Lily

Sepals

Sepals look like leaves. Sepals usually are green. But they can be other colors too. Sepals cover the flower bud before it opens. They fold back as the flower opens.

Photo: Fuchsia

Petals

Petals are colored flaps. They are under the sepals when the bud is closed. They open up when a flower blooms. Petals keep the parts inside the flower safe. Their color draws insects.

Photo: Asters

Some flowers have pockets
at the bottom of their petals.
These pockets hold nectar.
Nectar is a sweet liquid.
Some birds, butterflies, and
ants drink nectar.

Photo: Hibiscus

Pollen

Stamens

The stamens grow in a circle inside a flower blossom. The tops of the stamens hold pollen. Pollen looks like tiny pieces of sand or powder.

Photo: Center of a Tulip

Most pollen is yellow. Pollen can be sticky or dry. Pollen fertilizes flowers. A flower makes seeds if it is fertilized.

Photo: Center of a Prickly Pear Cactus Flower

Stigma
Pistil

Pollen needs to fall onto the pistil to fertilize a flower. The pistil looks like a small stem. The top of the pistil is the stigma. The stigma is sticky. Pollen sticks to the stigma and enters the pistil. The pistil holds tiny eggs inside. The eggs turn into seeds if they are fertilized.

Photo: Leopard Lily

A flower can fertilize itself. Its pollen needs to fall from its stamens onto its pistil. A flower can also fertilize another flower of the same kind. This happens if pollen spreads from flower to flower.

Photo: Sego Lily

Bees, butterflies, and flies carry pollen from flower to flower. The wind also carries pollen. Pollen helps flowers make seeds.

Photo: Purple Coneflower

Words to Know

bloom—to open up into a flower

fertilize—to start to grow a seed that will make a new plant

nectar—a sweet liquid inside a flower that butterflies, ants, and some birds drink

petal—one of the colored flaps or outer parts of a flower

pistil—a stem in the center of the flower; the pistil holds tiny eggs.

pollen—tiny pieces on top of stamens in a flower; pollen looks like sand or powder.

sepal—the part of the flower that covers the bud before it blooms

stamen—one of many stems inside a flower blossom

stigma—the top of the pistil; the stigma is sticky to catch pollen.

Read More

Barlowe, Dot. *Learning about Flowers.* Mineola, N.Y.: Dover Publications, Inc., 1997.

Bryant-Mole, Karen. *Flowers.* See for Yourself. Austin, Tex.: Raintree Steck-Vaughn, 1996.

Butler, Daphne. *What Happens When Flowers Grow.* What Happens When...? Austin, Texas: Raintree Steck-Vaughn, 1995.

Internet Sites

Flowers at Enchanted Learning
http://www.enchantedlearning.com/themes/flowers.shtml

Kid's Valley Garden
http://www.raw-connections.com/garden

What Is a Flower?
http://tqjunior.thinkquest.org/3715/flower.html?tqskip=1

Index/Word List

Word Count: 270
Early-Intervention Level: 23

Editorial Credits
Lois Wallentine, editor; James Franklin, designer; Michelle L. Norstad, photo researcher

Photo Credits
Chuck Place, 4, 14, 16
Dembinsky Photo Associates/Anthony Mercieca, 10; Adam Jones, 12; Skip Moody, 20
Images International/Bud Nielson, cover
Kay Shaw, 6
Michael Worthy, 18
Root Resources/Louise K. Broman, 8
Richard Hamilton Smith, 1

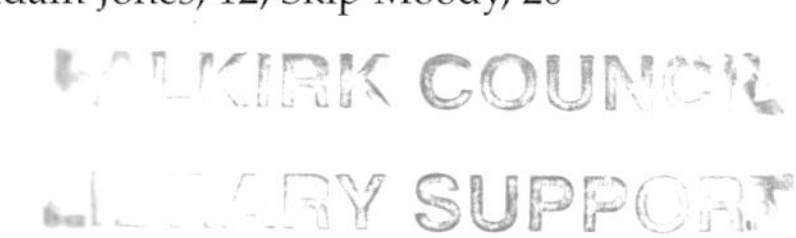